THE MUSLIM GIRL'S GUIDE TO ADOLESCENCE

Navigating Puberty with Faith for Ages 8-12

Practical Advice and Inspirational Guidance for Empowering Her Journey through Teenhood with Grace and Wisdom

Maryam Aisyah

Copyright © Maryam Aisyah, 2024.

All rights reserved. No part of this book may be reproduced, distributed, or transmitted in any form or by any means, including photocopying, recording, or other electronic or mechanical methods, without the prior written permission of the author, except in the case of brief quotations embodied in critical reviews and certain other noncommercial uses permitted by copyright law.

Table of contents

Introduction..3
Chapter 1:..8
Embracing Change.....................................8
Chapter 2:..17
Modesty and Awrah..................................17
Chapter 3:..26
The Spiritual Journey................................26
Chapter 4:..35
Understanding Menstruation....................35
Chapter 5:..45
Emotional Well-being...............................45
Chapter 6:..55
Cultivating Islamic Identity.......................55
Chapter 7:..65
Practical Guidance...................................65
Conclusion..74

Introduction

In the sacred journey of life, there comes a pivotal moment—a moment that heralds the blossoming of innocence into wisdom, of curiosity into understanding, of a child into a young woman. It's a moment whispered in the wind, sung by the stars, and cherished in the hearts of generations past. This moment is puberty.

But for the Muslim girl, puberty isn't just a biological phenomenon; it's a sacred milestone intricately woven into the tapestry of faith. It's a journey that transcends the physical realm, guiding her towards spiritual awakening and self-discovery. It's a journey that beckons her to embrace her identity, her beliefs, and her essence as a Muslimah.

In "The Muslim Girl's Guide to Adolescence: Navigating Puberty with Faith," we embark on a wondrous odyssey—a journey of exploration, empowerment, and enlightenment. With the Quran as our compass and the teachings of the Prophet

Muhammad (peace be upon him) as our guiding light, we navigate the turbulent waters of adolescence with grace, wisdom, and unwavering faith.

As we delve into the significance of puberty in Islam, we uncover the profound wisdom behind this sacred transition. We discover that puberty isn't just a biological process—it's a divine gift bestowed upon us by the Most Merciful, a testament to His infinite wisdom and boundless love. It's a journey of self-discovery, self-love, and self-acceptance—a journey that leads us closer to Allah and deeper into the depths of our souls.

With every turn of the page, we unravel the mysteries of adolescence, exploring the physical, emotional, and spiritual dimensions of this transformative period. We learn to embrace our changing bodies with gratitude and humility, recognizing them as vessels of divine grace and instruments of spiritual growth. We navigate the complexities of modesty and awrah with confidence and conviction, honoring the sacred boundaries set forth by our Creator.

But above all, we discover the power of faith—the unwavering faith that sustains us through the trials and tribulations of adolescence, the faith that empowers us to rise above the challenges and embrace the blessings of womanhood. For in the heart of every Muslim girl lies a flame—a flame of faith, of resilience, and of unwavering devotion to Allah.

So join us on this extraordinary journey—a journey of self-discovery, sisterhood, and spiritual transformation. Let us embark on this adventure together, hand in hand, heart in heart, as we navigate the wondrous terrain of adolescence with faith as our compass and Allah as our guide. For in the pages of this book, you will find not just words, but whispers of wisdom, echoes of enlightenment, and the timeless truths that illuminate the path of every Muslim girl.

Chapter 1:
Embracing Change

In the quiet moments of dawn, as the sun begins its ascent into the sky, something miraculous stirs within the depths of the human body—a silent symphony of growth, transformation, and renewal. This symphony is puberty—a time of profound biological changes that herald the transition from childhood to adulthood.

At the heart of puberty lies the endocrine system—a complex network of glands and hormones that orchestrates the body's development and growth. As puberty unfolds, these hormones surge like waves crashing upon the shore, triggering a cascade of changes that transform the body from within.

One of the most visible signs of puberty is the onset of physical growth—a sudden surge in height and weight that often catches girls by surprise. Overnight, it seems, they find themselves towering over their childhood selves, their limbs stretching towards the sky like branches reaching for the sun.

But it's not just their height that changes—every aspect of their body undergoes a metamorphosis. Their hips widen, their breasts develop, and their curves begin to take shape, transforming them from girls into young women.

Alongside these external changes, a myriad of internal transformations takes place. The ovaries awaken from their slumber, releasing eggs into the womb in preparation for potential motherhood. The uterus thickens, shedding its lining in a monthly dance of fertility and renewal. And the breasts, those symbols of femininity and nourishment, begin to swell with the promise of life.

But perhaps the most profound change of all is the awakening of desire—the stirring of newfound feelings and emotions that awaken within the depths of the heart. As girls navigate the tumultuous waters of puberty, they find themselves grappling with a whirlwind of emotions—from joy and excitement to confusion and uncertainty.

Yet amidst the chaos of change, there is beauty—a beauty that lies in the miracle of creation, the miracle of life unfolding before our very eyes. For puberty is not just a biological process—it's a testament to the awe-inspiring power of Allah, the Creator of all things great and small.

In the tapestry of adolescence, woven with threads of change and transformation, growth spurts and hormonal changes stand as pillars of this remarkable journey. Like the unfolding petals of a flower, these phenomena symbolize the blossoming of youth and the emergence of new beginnings.

With the advent of puberty, the body undergoes a remarkable growth spurt—a sudden surge in height and weight that seems to occur almost overnight. Girls find themselves outgrowing their clothes and shoes at an alarming rate, as if their bodies are in a race to catch up with the rapid pace of their maturing minds.

But growth spurts are not just physical—they're also accompanied by a flurry of hormonal changes that ripple through the body like waves upon the shore. Estrogen, the primary female sex hormone, floods the bloodstream, signaling the ovaries to begin their monthly dance of fertility. Progesterone, its faithful companion, follows close behind, preparing the womb for the possibility of new life.

Yet amidst the chaos of hormones and growth, there is beauty—a beauty that lies in the exquisite synchronicity of the human body, the delicate balance of nature's design. For each hormone serves a purpose, each growth spurt a testament to the miraculous journey of adolescence.

As girls navigate the ups and downs of puberty, they may find themselves grappling with a rollercoaster of emotions—from elation to frustration, from excitement to anxiety. Hormones, like unseen puppeteers, pull the strings of their hearts and minds, shaping their moods and influencing their thoughts.

But amidst the turbulence of adolescence, there is strength—a strength that lies in the resilience of the human spirit, the ability to weather the storms of change and emerge stronger on the other side. For growth spurts and hormonal changes are not just physical—they're also spiritual, emotional, and psychological, shaping the very essence of who we are.

So let us embrace these changes with grace and gratitude, knowing that they are a natural part of the journey towards womanhood. Let us celebrate the beauty of our bodies, our minds, and our souls, knowing that each growth spurt and hormonal change is a testament to the miracle of life itself. And let us embark on this journey of puberty with faith as our compass, trusting in Allah's plan for us and surrendering to the divine rhythm of growth and transformation.

In the tapestry of Islamic teachings, woven with threads of wisdom and compassion, lies a profound reverence for modesty and cleanliness—a reverence that extends to every aspect of a Muslim girl's life, especially during the transformative journey of puberty.

Modesty, in Islam, is not merely a matter of dress or appearance—it's a state of mind, a way of being that reflects humility, dignity, and respect for oneself and others. It's about cultivating a sense of inner beauty that radiates outward, adorning oneself with the garments of righteousness and piety.

At the heart of Islamic modesty lies the concept of awrah—the parts of the body that should be covered in front of others. For girls reaching puberty, this means dressing modestly and preserving their modesty in both their attire and their behavior. It means wearing loose-fitting clothing that conceals the shape of the body and observing proper etiquette in interactions with others.

But modesty goes beyond outward appearances—it's also about maintaining a clean and pure heart, free from the stains of arrogance, pride, and impurity. It's about purifying oneself spiritually and striving for excellence in all aspects of life, whether it be in prayer, in speech, or in conduct.

Cleanliness, too, holds a special place in Islam, as it is considered half of faith. From performing ablutions before prayer to observing proper hygiene practices, cleanliness is an integral part of a Muslim's daily life. And during puberty, it becomes even more important as girls navigate the physical and hormonal changes that accompany this stage of life.

As girls embark on the journey of puberty, they are reminded of the importance of modesty and cleanliness in Islam. They are encouraged to uphold these values with sincerity and devotion, knowing that they are not just outward rituals, but reflections of the purity and piety that lie within.

So let us embrace the teachings of Islam with open hearts and minds, striving to embody the virtues of modesty and cleanliness in our daily lives. Let us adorn ourselves with the garments of righteousness and piety, knowing that true beauty lies not in outward adornment, but in the purity of the soul. And let us journey through puberty with faith as our guide, trusting in Allah's wisdom and grace to illuminate our path.

Chapter 2:
Modesty and Awrah

In the intricate tapestry of Islamic teachings, the concept of modesty stands as a cornerstone—a timeless virtue that embodies humility, dignity, and reverence for oneself and others. Rooted in the teachings of the Quran and the traditions of the Prophet Muhammad (peace be upon him), modesty is more than just a set of rules or guidelines—it's a way of life, a spiritual journey that shapes the very essence of a Muslim's character.

At its core, modesty in Islam is about cultivating a sense of inner beauty that radiates outward—a beauty that transcends physical appearance and encompasses the purity of the heart and soul. It's about adorning oneself with the garments of righteousness and piety, striving to embody the virtues of humility, kindness, and selflessness in every thought, word, and deed.

For girls reaching puberty, modesty takes on added significance as they navigate the changes and challenges of adolescence. It becomes a guiding principle that shapes their choices and behaviors, guiding them towards a path of dignity and respect. From dressing modestly to observing proper etiquette in interactions with others, girls are encouraged to uphold the principles of modesty with sincerity and devotion.

But modesty in Islam is not just about external appearances—it's also about cultivating a sense of inner modesty, humility, and self-awareness. It's about recognizing the inherent worth and dignity of every individual, treating others with kindness and compassion, and striving to be the best versions of ourselves.

In the Quran, Allah commands believers, both men and women, to lower their gaze and guard their modesty, reminding them that true beauty lies not in outward adornment, but in the purity of the heart and soul. And in the example of the Prophet Muhammad (peace be upon him), we find the epitome of modesty—a man who exemplified humility, integrity, and grace in all aspects of his life.

In the delicate fabric of Islamic teachings, the rules of awrah serve as threads of guidance, weaving together notions of modesty, dignity, and respect. Awrah, referring to the parts of the body that should be covered in front of others, holds profound significance in Islam, especially for girls entering the transformative phase of puberty.

As young Muslimahs navigate the complexities of adolescence, they are entrusted with the sacred duty of upholding their modesty by adhering to the rules of awrah. These rules, rooted in the Quran and the traditions of the Prophet Muhammad (peace be upon him), provide clear guidance on how to dress and behave with dignity and respect.

For girls reaching puberty, the rules of awrah dictate that certain parts of the body should be covered in the presence of others, particularly those of the opposite gender who are not immediate family members. This includes covering the entire body except for the face, hands, and feet, as well as ensuring that clothing is loose-fitting and conceals the shape of the body.

But beyond the physical aspects of modesty, maintaining modesty also involves observing proper etiquette and behavior in interactions with others. It means speaking with kindness and respect, lowering one's gaze in the presence of the opposite gender, and avoiding situations that may compromise one's integrity and dignity.

In essence, the rules of awrah serve as a safeguard for preserving one's modesty and dignity in a world that often seeks to diminish them. By adhering to these rules, girls are empowered to navigate the challenges of adolescence with grace and integrity, knowing that they are upholding the timeless values of Islam.

So let us embrace the rules of awrah with humility and devotion, recognizing them not as restrictions, but as pathways to spiritual growth and self-respect. Let us adorn ourselves with the garments of modesty and dignity, knowing that true beauty lies not in outward appearance, but in the purity of the heart and soul.

As young Muslim girls embark on the journey of adolescence, navigating the terrain of puberty with faith as their compass, they are entrusted with the sacred duty of upholding their modesty and dignity in both dress and behavior. Here are some practical tips to guide them on this journey:

Dressing Modestly:
1. **Choose Loose-Fitting Clothing:** Opt for garments that are loose-fitting and do not cling to the body, allowing for freedom of movement while maintaining modesty.

2. **Cover the Awrah:** Ensure that the entire body is covered except for the face, hands, and feet in the presence of non-mahram (non-related) individuals.

3. **Select Modest Styles:** Look for clothing styles that provide adequate coverage, such as long sleeves, high necklines, and ankle-length skirts or pants.

4. **Use Layers:** Layering clothing can provide additional coverage and versatility, allowing for adjustment based on different situations and environments.

5. **Choose Appropriate Fabrics:** Opt for breathable, lightweight fabrics that provide comfort and modesty, such as cotton, linen, or jersey knit.

Behaving Modestly:
1. **Practice Modest Speech:** Speak with kindness, respect, and humility, avoiding coarse language or inappropriate topics of conversation.

2. **Lower Your Gaze:** Lower your gaze in the presence of the opposite gender, respecting their privacy and dignity.

3. **Maintain Proper Posture:** Stand and sit with dignity and grace, avoiding overly revealing or provocative body language.

4. **Respect Personal Space:** Respect the personal space and boundaries of others, refraining from physical contact that may be perceived as inappropriate.

5. **Avoid Immodest Behavior:** Refrain from engaging in behaviors that may compromise

your modesty or integrity, such as excessive flirting or immodest social media posts.

By incorporating these practical tips into their daily lives, young Muslim girls can navigate the challenges of adolescence with grace, dignity, and integrity, honoring the principles of modesty and respect that lie at the heart of their faith. Let us journey through puberty with faith as our guide, trusting in Allah's wisdom and grace to illuminate our path.

Chapter 3:
The Spiritual Journey

In the tapestry of life, faith serves as the golden thread that binds us to our Creator—a thread that weaves its way through the fabric of our existence, guiding us through the trials and tribulations of adolescence with unwavering strength and resilience.

For young Muslim girls embarking on the journey of puberty, faith is not just a concept—it's a lifeline, a source of solace and comfort in times of uncertainty and change. It's a beacon of hope that illuminates the path ahead, guiding them towards a deeper understanding of themselves and their purpose in this world.

At the heart of faith lies a profound connection to Allah—the Most Merciful, the Most Compassionate—the source of all guidance and wisdom. It is through this connection that young Muslim girls find strength in their moments of weakness, courage in their moments of fear, and peace in their moments of turmoil.

Through prayer, supplication, and remembrance, they cultivate a deep and intimate relationship with Allah, drawing closer to Him with each passing day. They find solace in the words of the Quran, finding guidance and inspiration in its timeless verses. They seek refuge in the example of the Prophet Muhammad (peace be upon him), emulating his noble character and righteous deeds.

But perhaps most importantly, they find comfort in the knowledge that they are never alone—that Allah is always with them, guiding them, protecting them, and showering them with His infinite mercy and grace. It is this unwavering faith and connection to Allah that sustains them through the trials and tribulations of adolescence, empowering them to face the challenges of puberty with courage, grace, and dignity.

So let us nurture our faith and strengthen our connection to Allah, knowing that He is the ultimate source of guidance and support in our journey through puberty and beyond. Let us seek solace in His presence, finding comfort in His love and mercy. And let us walk this path with faith as our guide, trusting in Allah's wisdom and grace to illuminate our way.

In the labyrinth of adolescence, where uncertainty and change often reign supreme, prayer and spiritual practices serve as anchors—steadfast reminders of our connection to Allah and the source of strength and guidance in times of turbulence.

For young Muslim girls navigating the tumultuous waters of puberty, prayer becomes more than just a ritual—it becomes a lifeline, a sanctuary of peace and tranquility amidst the chaos of adolescence. It's a time to seek solace in the presence of Allah, to pour out our hopes, fears, and dreams before Him, knowing that He listens with an ever-attentive ear and a heart full of compassion.

In the pre-dawn hours, as the world slumbers in silence, Muslim girls rise from their beds to perform the Fajr prayer—a sacred act of devotion that sets the tone for the day ahead. With each prostration, they find strength in their vulnerability, solace in their surrender, and courage in their submission to the will of Allah.

Throughout the day, they pause to perform the Zuhr, Asr, and Maghrib prayers—each one a precious opportunity to reconnect with their Creator, to seek His guidance and blessings, and to renew their faith and commitment to Him. In the rhythm of their prayers, they find comfort in the knowledge that Allah is always near, always listening, and always ready to answer their prayers.

But prayer is not just about words—it's also about actions. It's about embodying the teachings of Islam in every aspect of our lives, from our interactions with others to our treatment of the environment. It's about living with integrity, honesty, and compassion, knowing that our actions speak louder than words.

In addition to prayer, young Muslim girls engage in other spiritual practices during adolescence, such as reading the Quran, attending religious classes, and participating in community service activities. These practices not only deepen their connection to Allah but also strengthen their bonds with their faith community, fostering a sense of belonging and purpose in a world that often feels chaotic and uncertain.

So let us embrace prayer and spiritual practices as integral parts of our journey through adolescence, knowing that they are not just rituals, but pathways to spiritual growth and enlightenment. Let us seek solace in the presence of Allah, finding comfort in His love and guidance. And let us walk this path with faith as our guide, trusting in Allah's wisdom and grace to illuminate our way.

In the labyrinth of adolescence, where uncertainty and change often reign supreme, challenges abound, testing the limits of our faith and resilience. Yet, it is precisely in the face of these challenges that our faith shines brightest, illuminating the path ahead and guiding us through the darkest of times.

For young Muslim girls navigating the tumultuous waters of puberty, challenges come in many forms—physical, emotional, and spiritual. From the physical changes of puberty to the pressures of peer relationships and academic expectations, they find themselves grappling with a whirlwind of emotions, doubts, and uncertainties.

But amidst the chaos of adolescence, there is beauty—a beauty that lies in the resilience of the human spirit, the ability to rise above adversity and emerge stronger on the other side. It is through faith that young Muslim girls find the strength to face their challenges head-on, knowing that Allah is always by their side, guiding them, protecting them, and empowering them to overcome.

With unwavering faith as their compass and resilience as their shield, they navigate the trials and tribulations of adolescence with grace and dignity, trusting in Allah's plan for them and surrendering to His will. They draw strength from the words of the Quran, finding solace in its timeless wisdom and guidance. They seek inspiration from the example of the Prophet Muhammad (peace be upon him), emulating his courage, perseverance, and unwavering faith in the face of adversity.

But perhaps most importantly, they find comfort in the knowledge that they are not alone—that Allah is always with them, guiding them through the storms of life and leading them towards a brighter tomorrow. It is this unwavering faith and resilience that sustains them through the challenges of adolescence, empowering them to emerge stronger, wiser, and more resilient than ever before.

So let us embrace the challenges of adolescence with faith as our guide and resilience as our ally, knowing that with Allah's help, we can overcome any obstacle that stands in our way. Let us trust in His wisdom and grace to illuminate our path, knowing that He is the ultimate source of strength and guidance in our journey through life. And let us walk this path with faith and resilience as our constant companions, knowing that with Allah's help, we can weather any storm and emerge victorious in the end.

Chapter 4:
Understanding Menstruation

In the intricate tapestry of human biology, menstruation stands as a testament to the wondrous complexity of the female body—a natural process that signals the onset of fertility and the potential for new life.

Menstruation, often referred to as a period, is a monthly event that occurs in girls and women of reproductive age. It marks the shedding of the uterine lining, which occurs in response to changes in hormone levels within the body.

The menstrual cycle begins with the release of hormones from the brain's pituitary gland, signaling the ovaries to prepare for ovulation—the release of an egg. As the egg matures within the ovary, estrogen levels rise, triggering the thickening of the uterine lining in preparation for a potential pregnancy.

Around midway through the menstrual cycle, a surge in luteinizing hormone (LH) triggers ovulation, causing the mature egg to be released from the ovary into the fallopian tube. If the egg is not fertilized by sperm within a certain timeframe, it disintegrates, and estrogen and progesterone levels drop, signaling the body to shed the uterine lining.

This shedding of the uterine lining manifests as menstruation—a process characterized by the flow of blood and tissue from the uterus through the vagina. Menstrual blood may vary in color and consistency, ranging from bright red to dark brown and from light spotting to heavy flow, depending on individual factors such as hormonal fluctuations, diet, and overall health.

The menstrual cycle typically lasts around 28 days, although it can vary from person to person. Some girls and women may experience irregular periods or variations in cycle length, which can be influenced by factors such as stress, diet, exercise, and underlying health conditions.

While menstruation is a natural and normal part of the female reproductive cycle, it can also be accompanied by discomfort and symptoms such as cramps, bloating, mood swings, and fatigue. However, with proper self-care, including rest, hydration, and the use of heating pads or pain relievers, many girls and women are able to manage these symptoms and continue with their daily activities.

Overall, menstruation is a complex biological process that reflects the intricate interplay of hormones, organs, and systems within the female body. By understanding and embracing this natural phenomenon, girls and women can navigate the journey of menstruation with confidence, dignity, and grace.

In the teachings of Islam, cleanliness is not just a physical act—it's a spiritual practice, a reflection of purity and piety that extends to every aspect of a

Muslim's life. From the daily rituals of ablution to the meticulous observance of hygiene practices, cleanliness holds a special place in the hearts and minds of believers, guiding them towards a path of spiritual purity and enlightenment.

For young Muslim girls navigating the journey of puberty, hygiene practices and purity in Islam take on added significance as they embark on the sacred journey of womanhood. They are entrusted with the responsibility of upholding their cleanliness and purity, both inwardly and outwardly, as a reflection of their faith and devotion to Allah.

At the heart of Islamic hygiene practices lies the concept of taharah—a state of ritual purity that is attained through acts of cleansing and purification. This includes performing ablution before prayer, ensuring that the body and clothing are clean and free from impurities, and observing proper hygiene practices in all aspects of daily life.

In addition to physical cleanliness, Islam also emphasizes the importance of spiritual purity—the purification of the heart and soul from negative thoughts, feelings, and intentions. This involves seeking forgiveness for sins, repenting for wrongdoing, and striving to embody the virtues of compassion, kindness, and humility in all interactions with others.

During menstruation, young Muslim girls are taught to observe certain guidelines to maintain their purity and hygiene in accordance with Islamic teachings. This includes performing ghusl (ritual bath) after the end of menstruation, refraining from certain acts of worship such as prayer and fasting during menstruation, and observing proper hygiene practices to ensure cleanliness and purity throughout the menstrual cycle.

By embracing these hygiene practices and principles of purity, young Muslim girls not only uphold the teachings of Islam but also cultivate a deeper sense of connection to Allah and a greater awareness of their spiritual selves. They learn to view cleanliness not as a burden or chore but as a sacred duty and an opportunity for spiritual growth and purification.

So let us embrace the teachings of Islam with open hearts and minds, striving to embody the virtues of cleanliness and purity in our daily lives. Let us purify our hearts and souls, seeking forgiveness for our shortcomings and striving to live in accordance with the teachings of our faith. And let us journey through puberty with faith as our guide, trusting in Allah's wisdom and grace to illuminate our path.

Let's address some common questions and concerns that young Muslim girls may have during puberty, along with answers and guidance based on Islamic teachings:

Question: What is happening to my body during puberty, and why?

Answer: Puberty is a natural process of physical and hormonal changes that prepares your body for adulthood and reproduction. It's normal to experience growth spurts, changes in body shape, and the onset of menstruation for girls. These changes are driven by hormones produced by your body as it matures.

Question: How should I handle menstruation in Islam?

Answer: Menstruation is a natural part of a woman's life in Islam. During menstruation, you should continue to practice good hygiene, change sanitary products regularly, and maintain modesty in dress. However, certain acts of worship like prayer and fasting are temporarily paused until menstruation ends and a ritual bath (ghusl) is performed.

Question: How do I deal with emotions and mood swings during puberty?

Answer: Puberty can bring about intense emotions and mood swings due to hormonal changes. Remember that these feelings are normal and temporary. Turn to prayer, supplication, and seeking support from family and friends. Engage in activities that bring you joy and relaxation to help manage stress.

Question: What does Islam say about maintaining modesty during puberty?

Answer: Modesty is an important aspect of Islam, especially during puberty. This involves dressing modestly, covering the body appropriately, and observing proper behavior and etiquette. Remember to lower your gaze in the presence of the opposite gender and avoid situations that may compromise your modesty.

Question: How can I stay spiritually connected during puberty?

Answer: *Puberty is a time of spiritual growth and self-discovery. Nurture your faith through regular prayer, reading the Quran, and seeking knowledge about Islam. Surround yourself with positive influences and seek guidance from knowledgeable individuals when you have questions or concerns about your faith.*

Question: How do I maintain hygiene and purity during menstruation?

Answer: *It's important to maintain hygiene and purity during menstruation in Islam. Change sanitary products frequently, wash the genital area with water after using the bathroom, and perform ghusl (ritual bath) at the end of menstruation. Avoid intimate acts of worship like prayer and fasting until ghusl is performed.*

Chapter 5:
Emotional Well-being

Coping with stress and anxiety during puberty can be challenging, but with the guidance of Islam, young Muslim girls can find strength, resilience, and peace amidst the turmoil of adolescence. Here are some strategies rooted in Islamic teachings to help cope with stress and anxiety:

Turn to Prayer: Prayer is a powerful tool for managing stress and anxiety in Islam. Make time for regular prayer and turn to Allah in supplication, seeking His guidance, comfort, and support during times of difficulty. Remember that Allah is always near, ready to listen to your prayers and ease your burdens.

Practice Patience (Sabr): Patience is a virtue highly regarded in Islam, especially during times of adversity. Trust in Allah's plan for you and practice patience (sabr) in facing challenges and overcoming obstacles. Remember that difficulties are temporary and that Allah rewards those who persevere with patience and faith.

Seek Support from Family and Community: Reach out to trusted family members, friends, or members of your community for support and encouragement. Sharing your feelings and experiences with others can help alleviate feelings of isolation and provide a sense of connection and belonging.

Engage in Dhikr (Remembrance of Allah): Engage in dhikr, the remembrance of Allah, to calm your heart and soothe your soul. Recite verses from the Quran, engage in tasbih (repetitive praise of Allah), or simply reflect on the beauty of Allah's creation. Dhikr can help shift your focus away from stress and anxiety and towards gratitude and tranquility.

Take Care of Your Physical Health: Pay attention to your physical health by eating nutritious foods, getting regular exercise, and prioritizing sleep. A healthy body can better cope with stress and anxiety, and taking care of your physical health is an important part of maintaining overall well-being.

Practice Mindfulness and Reflection: Take time for self-reflection and introspection to better understand your thoughts, feelings, and reactions to stress. Practice mindfulness techniques such as deep breathing, meditation, or mindfulness exercises to calm your mind and increase your awareness of the present moment.

By incorporating these strategies into your life and relying on the teachings of Islam for guidance and support, you can cope with stress and anxiety during puberty with strength, resilience, and faith. Remember that Allah is with you every step of the way, guiding you through life's challenges and showering you with His mercy and grace. Trust in

Him, have patience, and never lose hope in His infinite wisdom and compassion.

Peer pressure and social challenges are common experiences during puberty, but young Muslim girls can navigate these obstacles with strength, confidence, and the guidance of Islam. Here are some strategies rooted in Islamic teachings to help cope with peer pressure and social challenges:

Stay True to Your Values: Islam teaches the importance of upholding one's values and principles, even in the face of peer pressure. Remember your beliefs and the teachings of Islam, and strive to stay true to them in all situations. Trust in Allah's guidance and find strength in your faith to resist negative influences.

Choose Your Friends Wisely: Surround yourself with friends who share your values and support your goals. Seek out positive influences and cultivate relationships with individuals who encourage you to be your best self. Remember that true friends will respect your beliefs and support you in your journey.

Set Boundaries: Establish clear boundaries for yourself and communicate them assertively with others. Learn to say no to activities or behaviors that go against your values or make you uncomfortable. Trust in your judgment and prioritize your well-being above social pressures.

Seek Guidance: Turn to trusted adults, such as parents, teachers, or mentors, for guidance and support when facing peer pressure or social challenges. Share your concerns openly and honestly with them, and seek their advice on how to navigate difficult situations in accordance with Islamic teachings.

Focus on Personal Development: Invest in personal growth and development by pursuing activities and interests that align with your values and aspirations. Engage in acts of worship, community service, or extracurricular activities that nurture your talents and passions, and contribute positively to your self-esteem and confidence.

Practice Self-Compassion: Be kind and compassionate towards yourself, especially during times of struggle or difficulty. Remember that everyone faces challenges in life, and it's okay to make mistakes or experience setbacks along the way. Treat yourself with love and forgiveness, and strive to learn and grow from every experience.

By incorporating these strategies into your life and relying on the teachings of Islam for guidance and support, you can navigate peer pressure and social challenges during puberty with grace, resilience, and faith. Remember that Allah is always with you, guiding you through life's ups and downs, and empowering you to overcome obstacles with strength and courage. Trust in Him, stay true to your values, and believe in yourself—you are capable of achieving great things, Insha'Allah.

Seeking support from family and community is essential for young Muslim girls navigating the challenges of puberty. Here are some ways they can seek and benefit from support:

Open Communication with Family: Foster open and honest communication with family members, including parents, siblings, and extended relatives. Share your thoughts, feelings, and concerns with them, and seek their advice and guidance on navigating puberty. Family members can offer support, understanding, and practical advice based on their own experiences and wisdom.

Building Trust: Build trust with your family members by demonstrating honesty, respect, and responsibility in your actions. Trust forms the foundation of strong family relationships and enables you to seek support and guidance without fear of judgment or criticism.

Seeking Guidance from Elders: Turn to elders and respected members of the community for guidance and wisdom. Elders often have valuable insights and life experiences to share, and their guidance can help you navigate challenges with grace and resilience.

Participating in Religious Communities: Engage with religious communities, such as mosques, Islamic centers, and youth groups, to connect with peers who share your faith and values. Participating in religious activities, events, and programs can provide a sense of belonging, support, and spiritual nourishment during puberty.

Mentorship and Role Models: Seek out mentors and positive role models within your family and community who can offer guidance, encouragement, and support. Mentors can provide valuable advice, share their own experiences, and serve as sources of inspiration and motivation as you navigate the journey of puberty.

Community Support Networks: Take advantage of community support networks and resources that are available to you. These may include counseling services, support groups, or educational programs focused on topics related to puberty, mental health, and personal development.

By seeking support from family and community, young Muslim girls can navigate the challenges of puberty with strength, resilience, and faith. Remember that you are not alone—there are people who care about you and are ready to support you every step of the way. Reach out, ask for help when you need it, and embrace the love and support of your family and community as you journey through adolescence.

Chapter 6:
Cultivating Islamic Identity

Nurturing faith, knowledge, and character is paramount for young Muslim girls embarking on the journey of puberty. It's a transformative period where they are not only experiencing physical changes but also shaping their identity and worldview. Through the lens of Islam, nurturing these aspects becomes a holistic endeavor, integrating spiritual, intellectual, and moral development seamlessly.

At the core of this nurturing process lies the strengthening of faith. For young Muslim girls, faith is more than a belief; it's a guiding light that illuminates their path through life's complexities. Through acts of worship such as prayer, recitation of the Quran, and supplication, they forge a deep connection with Allah, finding solace, guidance, and strength in their faith.

Simultaneously, nurturing knowledge is essential for empowering young Muslim girls to navigate the world with wisdom and discernment. Islamic education programs, Quranic study, and Hadith classes provide them with a solid foundation of Islamic knowledge, enabling them to understand and uphold the teachings of Islam in their daily lives. Encouraging critical thinking and reflection on religious and social issues equips them with the tools to navigate complex moral and ethical dilemmas.

As faith and knowledge intertwine, they give rise to character—the moral compass that guides young Muslim girls in their interactions with others and their choices in life. Embodying Islamic values such as compassion, honesty, and integrity, they become beacons of light in their communities, inspiring others through their words and actions. Through acts of charity, volunteering, and community service, they cultivate a sense of empathy and social responsibility, recognizing their role as stewards of Allah's creation.

In nurturing faith, knowledge, and character, young Muslim girls embark on a journey of self-discovery and growth, guided by the timeless teachings of Islam. With faith as their anchor, knowledge as their compass, and character as their beacon, they navigate the challenges of puberty with grace, resilience, and unwavering conviction. And as they journey through life, they continue to nurture these aspects, ever-striving to deepen their faith, expand their knowledge, and embody the values of Islam in all aspects of their lives.

Embracing cultural and religious heritage is a fundamental aspect of identity formation for young Muslim girls as they navigate the transformative journey of puberty. Rooted in rich traditions and timeless teachings, cultural and religious heritage serve as pillars of strength, resilience, and belonging, shaping their worldview and guiding their actions.

At the heart of embracing cultural and religious heritage is a deep appreciation for the diversity and richness of Muslim traditions and practices. From the vibrant tapestry of customs, rituals, and celebrations to the profound wisdom of Islamic teachings and scriptures, young Muslim girls are immersed in a heritage that spans centuries and continents, connecting them to their roots and identity.

Cultural heritage encompasses the customs, traditions, and practices passed down through generations, reflecting the unique identities and histories of Muslim communities around the world. Whether it's the colorful festivals of Eid, the cherished traditions of family gatherings and feasts, or the art, music, and literature that celebrate Muslim culture, young Muslim girls find joy, pride, and belonging in the cultural tapestry of their heritage.

Religious heritage, on the other hand, encompasses the spiritual teachings, values, and practices of Islam that form the foundation of Muslim identity. From the five pillars of Islam to the ethical principles outlined in the Quran and Hadith, religious heritage provides young Muslim girls with a moral compass and a sense of purpose, guiding them in their journey towards spiritual growth and enlightenment.

Embracing cultural and religious heritage is not just about preserving the past—it's about celebrating the richness of Muslim identity and finding meaning and connection in traditions that have stood the test of time. It's about instilling a sense of pride and belonging in young Muslim girls, empowering them to navigate the complexities of the modern world with confidence, dignity, and grace.

As young Muslim girls embrace their cultural and religious heritage, they cultivate a deep sense of identity, belonging, and purpose that serves as a source of strength and resilience in the face of adversity. They become ambassadors of their heritage, bridging cultures, fostering understanding, and spreading the beauty and wisdom of Islam to the world. And as they journey through puberty and beyond, they carry with them the rich tapestry of their heritage, guiding them in every step they take and shaping the legacy they leave behind.

As you journey through the exciting yet sometimes challenging phase of adolescence, it's important to embrace your Islamic identity with pride and confidence. Your identity as a young Muslim girl is a beautiful tapestry woven with faith, culture, and values that make you unique. Let's explore how you can strengthen this identity and navigate the world with grace and conviction.

Embracing Your Faith

In the bustling rhythm of life, it's easy to get swept away by the noise of the world. But amidst it all, your faith stands as a steadfast anchor, grounding you in times of uncertainty and guiding you towards the light. Embrace your faith with an open heart and a curious mind. Dive into the depths of Islamic teachings, exploring the Quran's timeless wisdom and drawing inspiration from the life of Prophet Muhammad (peace be upon him). As you deepen your understanding of Islam, you'll discover the beauty and richness of your faith, empowering you to walk with confidence in the path of righteousness.

Celebrating Your Heritage

Your cultural heritage is a vibrant tapestry woven with threads of tradition, customs, and stories passed down through generations. It's a mosaic of colors that reflect the beauty and diversity of the Muslim world. Take pride in your cultural identity, celebrating the festivals, rituals, and traditions that define who you are. Whether it's the joyous celebrations of Eid, the warmth of family gatherings, or the savory aromas of traditional cuisine, cherish the richness of your heritage and let it be a source of strength and joy in your journey.

Building Confidence

Confidence is not about being perfect; it's about embracing your flaws, owning your strengths, and stepping into your power with authenticity and courage. Believe in yourself and your abilities, knowing that you are capable of achieving greatness. Surround yourself with positivity and support, seeking guidance from mentors, family, and friends who uplift and empower you. Together, let's build a community of strong, confident Muslim girls who stand tall in the face of challenges and shine brightly with the light of faith.

As you embark on this journey of self-discovery and growth, remember that your Islamic identity is a beacon of light that illuminates your path. With pride in your heart and confidence in your step, you are ready to embrace the world with open arms and make a positive impact wherever you go. So go forth, dear sister, and shine your light brightly, for the world awaits the brilliance of your Islamic identity.

Chapter 7:
Practical Guidance

Navigating adolescence is a thrilling yet sometimes daunting adventure filled with twists, turns, and unexpected challenges. But fear not, dear sister, for you are not alone on this journey. Here are some tips and resources to guide you through the exhilarating ride of adolescence:

1. Embrace Your Uniqueness
Celebrate what makes you, YOU! Embrace your quirks, talents, and passions, and don't be afraid to shine brightly in the world.

2. Stay Connected to Your Faith
Keep your heart anchored in faith, and let it be your guiding light through life's ups and downs. Nurture your relationship with Allah through prayer, Quranic recitation, and acts of kindness.

3. Surround Yourself with Positive Influences

Choose friends who uplift and inspire you to be the best version of yourself. Surround yourself with people who share your values and support your dreams.

4. Take Care of Your Body and Mind
Prioritize your physical and mental well-being by eating healthily, staying active, and getting enough rest. Practice self-care activities that nourish your soul and rejuvenate your spirit.

5. Communicate Openly
Don't be afraid to speak up and share your thoughts, feelings, and concerns with trusted adults, whether it's your parents, teachers, or mentors. Communication is key to building strong relationships and navigating challenges together.

6. Seek Knowledge and Growth
Embrace the opportunity to learn and grow every day. Expand your horizons through reading,

exploring new hobbies, and seeking out opportunities for personal development.

7. Stay True to Yourself

Stay true to your values, beliefs, and aspirations, even in the face of peer pressure or societal expectations. Trust your instincts and follow the path that feels right for you.

Remember, dear sister, adolescence is a time of exploration, discovery, and growth. Embrace the journey with an open heart and a curious mind, knowing that each experience is a stepping stone towards becoming the confident, resilient woman you are meant to be.

Navigating adolescence can feel like embarking on a grand adventure, filled with excitement, challenges, and moments of self-discovery. To help you navigate this journey with confidence and grace, here are some practical tips and checklists to keep in mind:

Personal Hygiene Checklist:

☐ Shower or Bathe Daily: Keep your body clean and fresh by showering or bathing regularly, especially after physical activities.

☐ Brush Teeth Twice a Day: Maintain good oral hygiene by brushing your teeth in the morning and before bedtime.

☐ Wash Your Face: Cleanse your face twice daily to remove dirt, oil, and impurities.

☐ Change Clothes Regularly: Wear clean clothes and change your undergarments daily to stay comfortable and hygienic.

☐ Practice Menstrual Hygiene: During your period, change sanitary pads or tampons regularly and maintain proper menstrual hygiene.

Daily Routine Checklist:

☐ Morning Routine: Start your day with a healthy breakfast, pray Fajr, and set positive intentions for the day ahead.

☐ School or Study Time: Attend school or engage in educational activities to nurture your mind and intellect.

☐ Prayer and Reflection: Make time for regular prayer, Quranic recitation, and reflection on Islamic teachings.

☐ Physical Activity: Stay active by engaging in sports, exercise, or outdoor activities to keep your body strong and healthy.

☐ Quality Time with Family: Spend quality time with your family, sharing meals, conversations, and bonding experiences.

☐ Evening Routine: Wind down in the evening with evening prayer (Isha), relaxation activities, and preparation for bedtime.

Social Interaction Advice:

☐ Choose Positive Influences: Surround yourself with friends who uplift and inspire you to be your best self.

☐ Set Boundaries: Know your limits and set boundaries in your relationships to protect your emotional well-being.

☐ Communicate Openly: Be honest and open in your communication with friends and family, expressing your thoughts, feelings, and concerns.

☐ Handle Peer Pressure: Stand firm in your beliefs and values, and don't succumb to peer pressure that goes against your principles.

- [ ] Build Empathy: Practice empathy and kindness in your interactions with others, showing compassion and understanding towards their feelings and experiences.

Spiritual Growth Tips:

- [ ] Prayer and Worship: Establish a regular prayer routine and engage in acts of worship to strengthen your connection with Allah.

- [ ] Quranic Study: Dedicate time to reading, studying, and reflecting on the Quran to deepen your understanding of Islam.

- [ ] Seek Knowledge: Attend Islamic classes, seminars, or online courses to expand your knowledge of Islamic teachings and principles.

- [ ] Community Engagement: Get involved in community service projects, volunteer work, or youth groups to connect with other Muslims and make a positive impact in your community.

Emotional Well-being Strategies:

☐ Express Yourself: Find healthy ways to express your emotions, whether through journaling, art, or talking to a trusted friend or family member.

☐ Manage Stress: Practice stress-relief techniques such as deep breathing, mindfulness, or relaxation exercises to manage stress and anxiety.

☐ Seek Support: Don't hesitate to seek support from trusted adults, counselors, or mental health professionals if you're struggling with emotional difficulties or mental health issues.

By following these practical tips and checklists, you can navigate adolescence with confidence, resilience, and grace, embracing the journey of self-discovery and growth with open arms.

Conclusion

As we come to the end of our journey together, it's important to reflect on the empowering messages and guidance we've explored throughout this book. As young Muslimahs navigating the exciting yet sometimes challenging terrain of adolescence, you are embarking on a journey of self-discovery, growth, and empowerment.

Puberty is a significant milestone in your life—a time of physical, emotional, and spiritual transformation. Embrace this journey with an open heart and a curious mind, recognizing that it is a natural and beautiful part of your development as a young woman. Remember that Allah has created you perfectly, and each change you experience is a reflection of His wisdom and mercy.

As you navigate the ups and downs of adolescence, remember that you are strong, capable, and resilient. Draw strength from your faith, your family, and your community as you face challenges and embrace opportunities for growth. Trust in yourself and in Allah's plan for you, knowing that you have the inner strength and courage to overcome any obstacle that comes your way.

In the journey ahead, embrace your faith with pride and confidence, knowing that it is a source of guidance, comfort, and strength. Seek knowledge with eagerness and curiosity, recognizing that learning is a lifelong journey that enriches your mind and spirit. And above all, cultivate resilience in the face of adversity, knowing that every challenge you overcome makes you stronger and more resilient.

As you embark on the next chapter of your life, remember that you are not alone. You are part of a community of strong, courageous Muslimahs who are walking this journey alongside you. Together, let us embrace puberty as a natural and spiritual journey, empowering each other to navigate adolescence with confidence, grace, and resilience.

Printed in Great Britain
by Amazon